Connor Court Quarterly
Volume 16

Woke Capitalism and the Power of Ideas

Published by Connor Court Publishing Pty Ltd, 2023

CONNOR COURT PUBLISHING PTY LTD
PO Box 7257
Redland Bay QLD 4165
sales@connorcourt.com
www.connorcourtpublishing.com.au

ISBN: 9781922815736

Cover design by Ian James
Printed in Australia

PREVIOUS ISSUE OF

THE CONNOR COURT QUARTERLY

Volume 16

Educare, Educere, and Educatum

The chattering classes, whispering classes, bully-victims and cancel-culture: life and education in the politically correct era

Mark Lopez

Of Life and of Leadership
by Brendan Nelson

Reviewed by Aniello Iannuzzi

St Cardinal John Henry Newman College, Brisbane

Kenneth Crowther

F is for Fail

Colleen Harkin

Discipline Of Mind:
An Address To The Evening Classes

John Henry Newman

They're Your Children: Take the Lead on Their Education

Cheryl Lacey

From Rousseau to the World Economic Forum: Woke Capitalism and the Power of Ideas

Rick Brown

The Voice
Beware the Shiny Bauble

Robert Katter

Introduction

Since the political emergence of Donald Trump and the successful referendum in the United Kingdom on leaving the European Union, there has been a focus on the deep-seated divisions within Western societies.

The first sign of this phenomenon occurred in Australia in 1999 with the referendum on a republic. The results could not be explained in terms of party allegiance or ideological terms such as Left or Right.

Rather the best explanation is postcodes — the majority of voters in the inner, metropolitan suburbs voted yes and the majority of voters in the outer, metropolitan suburbs and the regional areas voted no.

It appears that similar analyses could be undertaken elsewhere. Wall Street, Silicon Valley and the northern parts of the east and west coasts oppose Mr. Trump with a venom. His support is in the South and mid-West.

A similar intensity of feeling recently has manifested itself with respect to Nigel Farage, to whom 'The City' attributes responsibility for the Brexit result. Again,

Brexit was a case of City's supporting the European Union and London's outer suburbs and cities such as Birmingham and Manchester opposing it.

Support for Marine Le Pen now has spread, but for many years in was centred in the north of France. And so it goes on.

The influence of the élites and their born-to-dictate mindset is now in our faces. This reinforces the depth of the gulf between the élites and to use Hiliary Clinton's famous term 'the deplorables'.

Society is being forced to accept what were not-so-long-ago radical ideas as normal and sensitive: gay marriage; transsexual people are entitled to play women's sport at an élite level and use women's bathrooms; there are more than 70 genders; teenagers ought to be able to change their sex if they feel like it; humans are destroying the earth which will cease to exist as we know it unless we take drastic action now.

These developments also provoke thought about whether the élites have re-emerged, never really gone away, or changed. Is the gulf between the élites and the masses wider than it used to be? After all, universal adult suffrage was supposed to deliver an egalitarian society.

Rick Brown seeks to grapple not only with what is happening but also why and how we got to where we are.

He thinks that political parties are not the explanation

for what is happening and are not the primary vehicle through which these challenges can be addressed.

Rather he is attracted to John Meynard Keynes observation that ‘the power of vested interest is vastly exaggerated when compared with the gradual encroachment of ideas’.

Brown’s prisms are the foundations of the ideas which drive society today, the transmission of those ideas and the rise of the current attitudes of the élites towards ‘the deplorables’.

His analysis is based on the proposition that what we are seeing now did not happen overnight and so in part, his essay is a history of the modern evolution of ideas and their transmission.

His story about the foundations of the ideas that drive the cultures of the inner metropolitan suburbs and outer suburbs takes us back more than 200 years to Jean Jacques Rousseau, who the late Sir Roger Scruton described as ‘the first and greatest of the liberal reformers whose impact on modern culture and modern politics has been equalled by no other thinker of the Enlightenment’. It also involves a Rousseau contemporary Edmund Burke, the founder of conservatism.

The transmission of these ideas he credits to the creator of cultural hegemony and Communist theoretician Antonio Gramsci, whose ideas and strategy have been sloganised as ‘the long march through the institutions’.

He also focuses on the dictatorial mindset of today's élites which is different from their recent predecessors and turns to the attitudes of America's founders who set out to prevent the creation of a fully democratic society and, at one level, to retain real power in the hands of their class.

To complete the picture, he turns a spotlight on Klaus Schwab, the owner of the World Economic Forum, who has persuaded the global business élite to impose management 'dictatorship' through a concept called 'stakeholder management'.

Robbie Katter is a third consecutive generation politician. If, as expected, he is re-elected next year, a Katter will have represented a part of North Queensland for 60 consecutive years. During all that time, the Katters have been vocal and active supporters of Aboriginal people and their advancement. Robbie's grandfather ended segregation in Cloncurry in the 1960s.

Robbie opposes 'The Voice'. His essay is a case study of the issues canvassed in Rick Brown's essay: people in the inner metropolitan suburbs in Sydney, Melbourne and Canberra, including middle-class Aboriginals, pontificating about the best interests of Aboriginals in regional and rural Australia.

He argues that if the 'The Voice' were passed it would not improve the circumstances, opportunities or lifestyles of the Aboriginals with whom he interacts on a daily basis. In fact, he said he could be counterproductive because passing the referendum could provide people with an excuse to say that they had fixed the Aboriginal issues and move on to the next cause.

He also highlights the hypocrisy of politicians who support The Voice, but oppose concrete, practical measures which could provide Aboriginals with opportunities and improve their lives.

Rick Brown's essay is confronting and challenging. However, there is good news. This year there are signs of green shoots of resistance through consumers applying their power and via élite sports players in the USA, people power in Europe, and most recently, the extraordinary Nigel Farage.

Just as the fact that there are people like Robbie Katter at the coalface gives cause for hope.

***

From Rousseau to the World Economic Forum: Woke Capitalism and the Power of Ideas

Rick Brown

Preamble

British TV presenter and leader of the Brexit campaign, Nigel Farage's recent experiences with the NatWest Bank and its subsidiary, the exclusive Coutts Bank; and his reception at Britain's Television and Radio Industry's awards in June, are metaphors for matters described in this essay.

They reflect the cultural transition since the 1950s and expose the elitism and born-to-dictate mindset of today's cultural and financial élites. The history extends from the 1700s with John Jacques Rousseau and with attitudes of America's founding élites towards democracy; through the defining of the English Establishment and the exposure of their class loyalties by *Spectator* columnist Henry Fairlie in the 1950s; Klaus Schwab's setting up, in the 1970s, an enterprise now known as the World Economic Forum as a vehicle to enable private corporations to become self-appointed "trustees of society". It continues with History Professor Christopher Lasch's putting a spotlight in the 1990s on the élites's contempt for the masses and their objective to erase any influence the masses might have by establishing parallel institutions to by-pass them; through to former Anheuser-Busch executive Anson Frericks's putting the spotlight on how BlackRock, Vanguard and State Street are driving 'woke' capitalism and the fruition of Mr. Schwab's dream of imposing 'stakeholder capitalism'; and on to Professor Carl Trueman's observation that, in an era in which the notion of assault on the person has become psychological, freedom of speech can be viewed as part of the problem rather than part of the solution.

The story about Mr. Farage's recent experiences, which appears towards the end of this essay, provides a real example of these developments and their consequences.

Introduction

This essay is founded on the following propositions:

- The power of vested interest is vastly exaggerated when compared with the gradual encroachment of ideas.
- Political parties are articulators of ideas rather than creators and incubators of ideas and have a minor role to play in cultural wars.
- Today, in the West, we live with the legacy of

Jean Jacques Rousseau, who died 240 years ago and who the late philosopher Sir Roger Scruton described as 'the first and greatest of the liberal reformers whose impact on modern culture and modern politics has been equalled by no other thinker of the Enlightenment'[1], and with the strategic brilliance of the leading Communist theoretician Italian Communist Party leader Antonio Gramsci who died more than 85 years ago.

- Milton Friedman's idea that there were only two economic models treated any form of intervention in the market as socialism, including conservatism which provides the philosophical foundation for the lifestyles and values of people living in the outer suburbs and regions.
- As the consequences of Mr. Friedman's doctrine such as the widening of the wealth gap and the social consequences of economic liberalism, became undeniable, 'stakeholder capitalism', a theory considered by some to constitute economic fascism, has become the dominant view among the financial ėlites
- The gulf between the views of the élites and those of the masses, which politically manifests itself in Australia as the chasm between the values and philosophies of residents of the inner suburbs and those of residents in the outer suburbs and regions,

1 'Rousseau & the origins of liberalism,' *The New Criterion*, October, 1998.

and which has been apparent since the Republic Referendum in 1999, is not a new phenomenon.

- As Rousseau's ideas have been described and developed and enhanced, liberalism or individualism or progressivism (which have the same foundations), have had consequences which he could not have envisaged.
- Gay marriage and transgenderism are not new cultural phenomena, but are the most recent symptoms of deep and long-established cultural pathologies in which the ideas of M. Rousseau play a prominent role.
- Similarly, what is called 'cancel culture', the erosion of the notion of the concept of truth, and freedom of speech's now being part of the problem, all begin with M. Rousseau's theory of self, a proposition which many people who consider themselves classic liberals, find confronting.

This essay seeks to build an understanding of the culture wars and the social divides which are engulfing both Australia and Anglo-Saxon countries and Western Europe generally through the prism of these propositions.

The Liberals

Earlier this year, Victorian Liberal MP Moira Deeming spoke at a rally organized by traditional feminists who believe that sex should not be determined by self-determined gender selection and that to do so threatens the identity of women.

The main speaker was British activist Kellie Jay Keen whose Wikipedia entry contains false information not provided by her.

The rally was gate-crashed by members of a neo-Nazi group, the National Socialist Network but initial media reported them as linked to the rally.[2]

The Liberals Victorian leader John Pesutto, a lawyer, accused Ms. Deeming of condoning Nazis and associating with extremists and told her to sign a letter disavowing Naziism and Ms. Keen.

He then sought to have her expelled from the parliamentary Liberal Party because she '*conduct(ed) activities in a manner likely to bring discredit on the Parliament or the Parliamentary Party*'. The basis of his actions was guilt by association and false information in a Wikipedia entry. There was no semblance of natural justice: innocent until proven guilty, due process and decisions based on verifiable evidence — once considered principles valued by the Liberals.

Mr. Pesutto is '*determined to lead a Liberal Party that is modern, it's contemporary, it's mainstream, it's inclusive and welcoming of everyone*'.[3] Yet, even though the rally was

2 For example, 'Liberal MP Moira Demming faces expulsion after neo-Nazi rally', *The Herald Sun*, Shannon Deary, 20th March, 2023.

3 'Moira Deeming was given three options. That's when the quarrel began'. *The Age*. Michael Bachelard and Sumeryya Ilanbey, 25th March, 2023.

about transgender issues, a 'Victorian Liberals insider' told Murdoch journalist Holly Hayes:

> *Ms Deeming's hard-line stances on social issues is hindering the embattled party from gaining more centrist voters.*
>
> *At end of the day, an MP is a brand ambassador for a political party.*
>
> *If you're joining the Liberal Party to implement regressive politics such as repealing abortion or turning back voluntary assisted dying, it's not the party for you.*[4]

The totalitarian approach of the Victorian Liberals appears to be at odds with the Liberal Party's principles and values as John Howard-era Foreign Minister Alexander Downer understands them. Last December he wrote:

> *From the 1949 election until the demise of the Howard government, people knew (the Liberal Party's) core values, which they associated with freedom to choose 'The public also knew the Liberal Party was the party of free speech and free expression, and that it believed in economic competition and debate about everything, from science to literature.*[5]

Ms. Deeming believed that at the party meeting it was agreed that she and Mr. Pesutto would issue a joint statement making it clear she had not been accused of

---

4 'Victorian Liberals decide MP Moira Deeming's future in party room vote', *news.com.au*, 27th March, 2023.

5 'Liberal Party must unashamedly articulate its timeless values', *Australian Financial Review*, 4th December, 2022.

being a Nazi or sympathiser and that her re-admission to the Parliamentary Party after her suspension would be automatic. Minutes of the meeting were cited to support this view.

Mr. Pesutto refused to issue a statement and made clear that her reinstatement was far from automatic. Consequently, Ms. Deeming made a fatal miscalculation. To apply pressure to Mr. Pesutto she threatened to sue him for defamation. That provided the opportunity to expel her from the parliamentary party.

The Secretary to the Parliamentary Party, Renee Health, also lost her job in the fallout. The minutes had to be discredited. Ms. Heath had to go. She had incurred the wrath of former leader Matthew Guy before she even had been elected. Mr. Guy reacted to claims that Ms. Heath, a Christian and the daughter of a Pentecostal minister, had benefited from branch stacking, by saying that she would not be allowed to be a member of the Parliamentary Party.

Australian Rules Football

The actions of the Victorian Liberals are not dissimilar to what has occurred in the Australian Rules football world. Last year the Hawthorn Football Club hired a consultant to report on the Club's relationships and interactions with its Aboriginal players from 2008 to 2016. The report contained some dramatic and appalling accusations.

The consultant did not speak to the people against whom these accusations were made and the Club did not speak to them after it received the report. Instead, it gave to the Australian Football League (AFL) the report which immediately found its way to the ABC.

The AFL appointed a panel headed by a QC to investigate the report. Eight months later the AFL wound it up. Some of the people who made accusations declined to participate in the review. Others declined to allow people against whom they made accusations to see documents related to the accusations.

The people against whom the accusations were made were named publicly, but the people making the accusations were not. The accused all denied the accusations, but, after eight months, they had not been spoken to by the Club, the AFL Commission or the Panel when it wound up.

The toll on one of those named Alister Clarkson, the coach of Hawthorn at the time and now the coach at another club was such that he stood down as coach because of his mental state for 11 weeks.

As with the Victorian Liberals, it is a case of self-described élite sporting bodies, which pontificate about their professionalism and pride themselves on being at the forefront of political correctness, ignoring the principles of natural justice, the concept of 'innocent until proven guilty' and evidence-based decision making. Former Hawthorn Football Club welfare manager Jason Burt thinks that '*the AFL is a brand. For them to say they're worried about people is false. It's all about brand.*'[6]

The Floating of the Australian Dollar

It might be asked how the Liberal Party in Victoria has gone from being a party, according to Mr. Downer, which '*for many years dominated the values debate in Australia*' and which was '*the party of free speech and free expression*'[7] to a reactionary party, captive to the woke agenda of inner metropolitan élites in which a person cannot '*have an idea or a difference of opinions without having eyes rolled, and nasty and personal interjections.*'[8]

What both Victorian politics and the AFL demonstrate is the power of ideas. It would be difficult to put a cigarette paper between Labor, the Victorian Liberals and the AFL in terms of their determination to be zealous champions of political correctness and the woke agenda.

Given the seismic nature of the transformation of the Victorian Liberals, at least, Mr. Downer's perception of the Liberal Party as a generator of ideas invites examination.

On that note, it is interesting that one question which never has been asked is how a solicitor with limited

6 'I've got nothing to say sorry for: Jason Burt responds to Hawthorn allegations,' *The Age,* 27th May 2022, Jack Niall.
7 'Liberal Party must unashamedly articulate its timeless values'.
8 'Victorian Liberal leader John Pesutto accused of bullying Renee Heath, as Moira Deeming fallout continues'.

commercial experience, Liberal John Howard, and a rock band manager, Labor Paul Keating, both became economic gurus and both championed the same ideology shortly after becoming federal treasurer.

Within weeks, if not days, of becoming Treasurer, the rock band manager had been convinced by the Reserve Bank Governor, Bob Johnston, appointed by his predecessor Mr. Howard, of the virtues of floating the Australian dollar and, with that, the surrendering of the Reserve Bank's ability to control the amount of cash in money markets.

While Mr. Keating got the prize for the treasurer who oversaw the floating of the dollar, the prize for being the person who paved the way for this decision is claimed also by Mr. Howard who established the Committee of Inquiry into the Australian Financial System (Campbell Committee) which recommended it.

However, various people have taken credit for these events. Dr. John Hewson, who was an adviser to Mr. Howard, having been an economist with the Reserve Bank and the International Monetary Fund, has taken credit for the decision to form the Campbell Committee.[9]

Mr. Hawke claimed that his office in which was ensconced economist Dr. Ross Garnaut was the engine room driving economic change.[10]

---

9 'Financial Deregulation in Australia', Ann Nevile, *The Economic and Labour Relations Review*, Volume 8, Issue 2, p. 276.

10 *The Hawke Memoirs* (William Heinemann, 1994), pp. 237-38.

It would appear then that neither Mr. Howard nor Mr. Keating played a significant role in the decision to float the dollar which has underpinned Australia's economic liberal agenda.

In fact, the Research Department of the Reserve Bank and in particular the Head of Research in the early 1970s Austin Holmes, whose name has not been mentioned, is best positioned to claim the credit.[11]

The Power of Ideas

The adoption by the major political parties of economic liberalism in the early 1980s, and, now their backing of the cultural agenda of inner metropolitan élites (including readiness to enforce adherence to this agenda with the zealotry of an ideologically fascist approach), demonstrate that power lies in ideas and with their promoters, and not with those who regurgitate them. The capitulation of the major political parties to noisy pressure groups and the reliance on the, often unconsciously biased, interpretation of focus group discussions reflects this reality.

Even then, the path from economic liberalism to the 'woke' agenda may not be as contradictory philosophically as it seems. Both have a common foundation: that of individualism, although economic liberalism did not imbibe the idea that feelings should dominate decision-making.

11 'The Mysteries of the Floating Dollar', P. D. Johnson, *Quadrant Online,* 1st April 2012.

Further, with the demise of conservatism and the ascendancy of liberalism, the major parties, in particular, have degenerated, to use the words of Wran Government Education Minister, Rod Cavalier, into '*executive placement agencies*' — '*divisions are not about ideas or ideology*'.[12]

The fact that the major political parties are regurgitators rather than incubators or creators of ideas, contrary to the belief of Mr. Downer, highlights the importance of an insight of an eminent economist John Meynard Keynes. In the last chapter of his treatise *The General Theory of Employment, Interest and Money*, published in 1936, he wrote:

> *The power of vested interests is vastly exaggerated compared with the gradual encroachment of ideas . (S)oon or late, it is ideas, not vested interests, which are dangerous for good or evil.*[13]

Power rests in ideas, not with their advocates.

With the proportion of voters in Australia not voting for the major parties rising to around 30 per cent, even the major parties cannot deny the gulf between the beliefs and values of inner metropolitan élites and those of the masses. Yet, both the major parties remain steadfast in their support of the agenda of these élites, even though they constitute a minority of the population, thereby demonstrating Mr. Keynes' proposition.

---

12 'Could Chifley Win Pre-selection today?', *Sydney Morning Herald*, 21st April 2005.

13 *The General Theory of Employment, Interest and Money*, Chapter 24, pp. 383-384.

The Establishment

The fact that these élites believe that they are entitled to ride roughshod over the majority and impose their opinions and values through bribery, intimidation or persecution, if necessary, should not be a surprise. A Professor of History at the University of Rochester, the late Christopher Lasch, pointed out almost 30 years ago, the contempt that the élites have for the concept of democracy as understood since the advent of universal adult franchise when he wrote:

> *The culture wars that have convulsed America since the sixties are best understood as a form of class warfare, in which an enlightened elite (as it thinks of itself) seeks not so much to impose its values on the majority (a majority perceived as incorrigibly racist, sexist, provincial, and /xenophobic), much less persuade the majority by means of rational public debate, as to create parallel or "alternative" institutions in which it will no longer be necessary to confront the unenlightened at all.*[14]

Almost ten years later British columnist Owen Jones made a similar observation about British society when he wrote:

> *Today's 'Establishment is made up – as it has always been – of powerful groups that need to protect their position in a democracy in which almost the entire adult population has the right to vote. The Establishment represents an attempt on behalf of*

14 'Introduction: The Democratic Malaise', *Revolt of the Elites and the Betrayal of Democracy* (New York, W.W. Norton and Company, 1995), pp. 20-21.

> *these groups to `manage' democracy, to make sure that it does not threaten their own interests. In this respect, it might be seen as a firewall that insulates them from the wider population.*[15]

Arguably the gulf between the self-appointed élites and the masses has been present since time immemorial. The social and economic divisions in society in Europe down the centuries are a matter of record and the French Revolution was a manifestation of them.

However, there is a perception that the USA was supposed to be different. However, a Professor of History at St. Louis University, the late James Hitchcock wrote that:

> *(i)f the elite group of Founding Fathers had been representative of public opinion in 1789, America would have developed as a secular state. There was, however, a wide gap between them and the masses of people; Enlightenment ideas usually spread only among a small minority.*[16]

Libertŭ, ŭgalitŭ, fraternitŭ did not translate to enthusiasm for universal, adult suffrage or even democracy. Speaking about the terms of senators, James Madison, who drafted the US constitution, said:

> *In England, at this day, if elections were open to all classes of people, the property of the landed proprietors would be insecure. (Governments)*

15 *The Establishment and how it works* (Allen Lane, London, 2014), Owen Jones, p.4.

16 *What is Secular Humanism* (Servant Books, Ann Arbor, Michigan, 1982), p. 52.

> *ought to be so constituted as to protect the minority of the opulent against the majority.*[17]

Thus, the USA consciously was formed as a republic not a democracy, a difference being, as Mr. Madison argued, that in a republic government is delegated to a small number of people,

> *whose wisdom may best discern the true interest of their country . (I)t may well happen that the public voice, pronounced by the representatives of the people, will be more consonant to the public good than if pronounced by the people themselves.*[18]

Alexander Hamilton (to whom the Democratic Party's roots can be traced) did not even have faith in 'the public voice':

> *All communities divide themselves into the few and the many. The first are the rich and well born, the other the mass of the people. They seldom judge or determine right. Give therefore to the first class a distinct, permanent share in the government. Nothing but a permanent body can check the imprudence of democracy.*[19]

It should not be surprising that 200 years later, founder of *The Weekly Standard*, Bill Kristol, told *Washington Post* journalist Greg Sargent, who described him as '*a fixture in the elite conservative and neoconservative establishments for*

17 *Notes of the Secret Debates of the Federal Convention of 1787*, Robert Yates Chief Justice of the State of New York, 26th June 1787.

18 'The Union as a Safeguard against Domestic Faction and Insurrection,' *The New York Packet*, 23rd November 1787.

19 *Notes of the Secret Debates*, 18th June 1787.

decades':

> *the party was more oligarchic than I realized. One always knew that the Republican Party was the party of business and therefore of the wealthy.*
>
> *Having said that, the degree of plutocracy, oligarchy – whatever the right word is – the degree of that was greater than I realized at the time.*[20]

As for Europe, *Spectator* columnist Henry Fairlie's description of 'The Establishment' in 1955 no doubt could be applied well beyond the boundaries of England:

> *By the 'Establishment' I do not mean only the centres of official power – though they are certainly part of it – but rather the whole matrix of official and social relations within which power is exercised. The exercise of power in Britain (more specifically, in England) cannot be understood unless it is recognised that it is exercised socially. the 'Establishment' can be seen at work in the activities of, not only the Prime Minister, the Archbishop of Canterbury and the Earl Marshal, but of such lesser mortals as the chairman of the Arts Council, the Director-General of the BBC, and even the editor of The Times Literary Supplement...*[21]

---

20 'A longtime conservative insider warns: the GOP can't be saved', *The Washington Post*, 6th September 2022.

21 'Political Commentary', *The Spectator*, 23rd September 1955, p. 5.

The Masses Revolt

Towards the end of the 20th century, this gulf was less apparent. This was due to the trappings of democracy associated with the universal adult franchise and the emergence of communism in the western world from the late 1930s to the end of the 1980s. The threat posed by communism created a form of social consensus against a common enemy.

During the 1980s liberalism, especially in economic policy, took hold in Anglo-Saxon countries in particular, and Western European countries to varying degrees. The extent of its penetration — all major political parties, the bureaucracy at all levels, the media, the professional classes — again demonstrates Mr. Keynes' proposition. However, as the 21st century has unfolded, the collapse of communism has exposed the incompatibility of conservatism — which accepts the notion of limits and asserts that the groups such as the family, community, nation, are the primary social units - with liberalism, which asserts that the individual is the primary social unit and does not accept the notion of limits. The consequences of the destruction of social structures, and the widening wealth gap wrought by this economic theory have focused attention on the gap between the élites and the masses.[22]

An analysis by the research Director of the European

22 A Tale of Two Nations (https://philosophymatters.substack.com/p/a-tale-of-two-nations).

Council on Foreign Relations Jeremy Shapiro of the vote on Brexit highlights the consternation of the élites that the established order and the legitimacy of their power is under a spotlight:

> *It is, after all, rather extraordinary that more than half the voting population defied a large majority of its own elected parliament, all of the traditional political parties, and virtually every important institution in the country – from the Central Bank to the leaders of industry to the trade unions.*
>
> *The elite political class's intellectual arguments failed to resonate with large segments of British society because they misread the country. They apparently believed that the same arguments that appealed to the younger, wealthier urban classes in London and Scotland would be sufficient to convince the rest of Britain of the value of the EU.*
>
> *In retrospect, they failed to fully appreciate the anger and frustrations of a huge swath of Britain.*
>
> *'For those people, the views and opinions of Treasury officials, prime ministers, and foreign leaders weren't just unconvincing – they were part of the problem.*[23]

The Brexit result demonstrated the power of ideas. It was not an institutional contest between political parties or capital against workers, but between the '*governing and the governed*', to use Mr. Shapiro's words, or the latest, self-appointed born-to-rule and the masses.

---

23 'Brexit was a rejection of Britain's governing élites. Too bad the élitess were right', *Vox*, Jeremy Shapiro, 25th June 2016.

Mr. Shapiro said that the élites would have to find *"a way to validate the concerns of their constituents on issues such as immigration and economic security without gutting their own principles*'. Otherwise, he said, 'the élites will really know what it's like to be governed by people who don't care about your concerns'.

Seven years later, with Marine le Pen's National Rally having 89 members in France's National Assembly, immigration is a hot-button issue. With more than 70 percent of respondents to an Oxoda-Backbone poll[24] conducted in May supporting both a referendum on immigration and backing quotas, the major parties are battling to find a response which will keep National Rally at bay.

Next Germany

In June, hot on the heels of the poll in France, a candidate of the Alternative für Deutschland (AfD) party, which rejects the climate change agenda and opposes immigration, defeated the Christian Democrat district administrator in Sonneberg, East Germany.

AfD campaigned on national issues, not local issues. The immigration level is at its highest since former chancellor Angela Merkel opened the floodgates in 2015. A report on the German news outlet *Welt*, showed that a large majority of the population thinks that politics is paying too little attention to the problems

24 'Immigration: les Franais soutiennet largement les propositions formulées par LR', *Le Figaro*, Dinah Cohen, 24th May 2023.

caused by immigration and only a few credit political parties with the competence to address this issue.[25]

Nevertheless, on the Friday before the Sonneberg election, and even though the Labour Minister Hubertus Hell has admitted that about 1.6 million Germans aged between 20 and 30 do not have a vocational qualification and '*all too often these people end up in long term unemployment*',[26] the Government passed legislation making it easier both for people outside the European Union to migrate to Germany and for asylum seekers resident in Germany before April to obtain skilled worker permits to get jobs without leaving Germany. Migrants seeking jobs will not necessarily have to be able to speak German. Parents and step-parents of skilled workers will be able to obtain residence permits.

Changes to the citizenship law will be made also. Dual and multiple citizenship will be allowed and the residence qualifying period will be reduced.

The views of the masses were ignored as the Government enacted the agenda of Big Business. In an ironic sign of the times, a government which includes the Social Democrats, the equivalent of the Labor Party in Australia, and the Greens delivered Big Business its agenda, while the major parties historically

---

25 'Mehrheit' sieht eher Nachteile von Zuwanderung – und will weniger Migranten aufnehmen' (Majority sees more disadvantages of immigration and wants to take in fewer migrants), *Welt*, 5th May 2023, Sabine Menkens.

26 'Germany looks to immigration reform to arrest worsening skill shortage'. *Financial Times*, 2nd May 2023, Guy Chazan.

associated with Big Business in Germany, the Christian Democratic Party and the Christian Social Union, voted against the legislation.

What would appear to be strange bedfellows and shifting alliances is a demonstration of the fact that, as in Australia, the major political parties in Germany are neither incubators nor creators of, nor even believers in ideas. At best, they are endorsers of, or reactors to ideas and, at worst, enforcers.

The German Government also proposes to ban gas and oil heaters in buildings from 2024 although, to the fury of the Greens, following poor results in recent state elections, one of the government parties, the Free Democratic Party, blocked the introduction of the legislation in May. The heat pumps required to replace the heaters could cost up to €20,000 more per installation than gas heating.

A week after the Sonneberg result, an AfD candidate was elected the fulltime mayor of Raguhn-Jessnitz in Saxony-Anhalt, the first time that an AfD candidate has won a fulltime mayoral position.

Twelve months ago, Germany's Greens' leader, Robert Habeck, led in popularity polls. Now a recent poll found that half of all Germans want him to resign. Support for the Greens has fallen from 23 per cent to 14 per cent as support for AfD has risen to 18 per cent.[27]

---

27 'From Hero to Zero: Robert Habeck picks up the climate tab' Hans von der Burchard and Gabriel Rialdi, *Politico*, 1st June 2023.

The German élites were apoplectic about the Sonneberg result. However, that did not lead to a discussion about the merit of the policies which caused it. The response of Germany's equivalent to ASIO, the BfV, to increased public support for the AfD, appeared to be to double down on its rhetoric about the threat of extremism, particularly from the 'far right'.

In June, before the Sonneberg result, the German Institute for Human Rights suggested that AfD was such a danger to democracy that it could be banned by Germany's Federal Constitutional Court.[28] Since then, as support for AfD has increased, the comments of German President Frank-Walter Steinmeier, whose role is to remain above politics, in a speech to Germany's domestic intelligence agency that 'we all have it in our hands to put those who despise our democracy in their place' have being interpreted as a veiled threat to AfD.[29] This followed an editorial of Der Spiegel calling for a banning of AfD two days earlier.

Perhaps this is not surprising when the BBC asserted, despite the *Welt* report, that '*the AfD does not reflect mainstream society's view that Germany needs migrant workers. But despite this, or maybe because of it, the party is reaching unprecedented numbers in the polls*'.[30]

The élites in Germany, and elsewhere, have profited

---

28 Voraussetzungen für Verbot der AfD erfüllt, Deutsches Institut für menschenrechte, 7th June 2023

29 'Germany considers ban on far-Right AfD', *The Telegraph*, James Jackson, 13th August 2023.

30 'Germany passes law to attract skilled migrant workers amid fierce debate' *BBC News*, 23rd June 2023, Damien McGuinness.

since the 1970s from the growth in the level of consumption driven by the expansion of the workforce, which appeared to develop out of the promotion of personal liberty in the 1960s. However, as they confront a consequence of that expansion — the long-term effect of declining birth rates and, therefore, now a shrinking domestic workforce — they are intent on ignoring the masses.

This response is an example of Mr. Lasch's observation that the élites have been creating parallel or 'alternative' institutions to avoid confronting 'the unenlightened'. This strategy is becoming more apparent as their ability to exercise control and influence surreptitiously has diminished. The facade of government of the people, by the people and for the people has given way to dismissing the views of the masses or, as in the case of the BBC assertion, putting a view that denies the facts, and relying on falsehood to justify a particular set of beliefs or interests.

Now England. More to Come?

In July there were three by-elections in England in safe Conservative Party seats. Labour overturned a 20,000 vote Conservative Party majority in Selby and Ainsty in North Yorkshire, although its own vote increased only by about 2,600 votes. In Somerset, the Liberal Democrats ousted the Conservative Party candidate with a 29 per cent swing away from the Conservative Party.

However, in Boris Johnson's former seat in west London, the Conservative Party hung on, despite expectations. Labour's leader Keir Starmer attributed the result there to the extension (by the Labour Mayor of London) of Ulez (Ultra Low Emission Zone) which imposes a fee on older and higher polluting vehicles, from inner London to the outer boroughs. He said that '*we are doing something very wrong if policies put forward by the Labour party end up on each and every Tory leaflet*.'[31]

The fact that Ulez was the brainchild of a Conservative Party politician — Boris Johnson no less — when he was the mayor of London did not cut ice. The less well-healed masses are not willing to bear the costs of a policy that the well-heeled élites wanted to impose on them. It was seen as Labour's London Mayor's determination to inflict on the equivalent of Australia's outer suburbs, a policy – Ulez – to drive his environment agenda.

Then there is Belgium which is an artificial construct comprising Dutch-speaking Flanders and French-speaking Wallonia. A party which supports the secession of Flanders, Vlaams Belang, aspires to be the largest party after the elections in June next year. According to Brussels-based *Politico* correspondent, Barbara Moens, that could provide it with the opportunity it seeks.

31 'Starmer says Labour doing something "very wrong" after Ulez-inked Uxbridge loss', *The Guardian,* Donna Ferguson and Tobi Thomas, 22nd July 2023.

If such an eventuality came to pass, it would be on the back of immigration and not secession which is its primary focus. The migrant influx is comparable to 2015. Ms. Moens says that migration is the biggest concern for voters and, in the opinion of an associate professor at the University of Ghent, Nicola Bouteca '*Vlams Belang owns the migration theme. That is the main reason for their success.*'[32]

The president of the second largest party in Flanders, Nieuw-Vlaamse Alliantie (*N-VA*), says that there is '*a wave of tremendous unease*'. People feel '*economically abandoned by their own elites*'.

Fascist Mindset?

In June, without offering an explanation, the Queensland Children's Hospital suspended a senior child psychiatrist, Dr. Jillian Spencer, over her approach to transgender patients. Dr. Spencer is a signatory to the National Association of Practising Psychiatrists' guide to managing gender dysphoria and incongruence in young people, which advocates a cautious approach and comprehensive mental health assessment. She is concerned that:

> *anyone's child will be encouraged at school, online, during extra-curricular activities, by their friends and by health professionals to contemplate their gender.*

32 'Why Belgium might be about to break up', *Politico*, 21st July 2023.

> *Even little kids are being encouraged to contemplate their gender.*
>
> *(F)amilies slowly come to realise that there is collusion going on between teachers, health professionals, child protection services and even the courts to ensure that all children are 'affirmed' even if their parents disagree with that approach.*[33]

Unlike Dr. Spencer, the Queensland Children's Hospital has a radical and aggressive policy to treating gender dysphoria. In 2022 it issued double the number of cross-sex hormones prescriptions that the Melbourne Children's Hospital gender clinic did.

Dr. Spencer has lodged a complaint with the Queensland Human Rights Commission about the actions of the Queensland Children's Hospital in suspending her.

She is not the only doctor concerned about the haste of the radicals taking a child's expressed gender identity as the starting point for treatment and promoting options, such as the use of puberty blockers, which have lifelong consequences.

The British National Health Service has commissioned an experienced paediatrician and former president of the Royal College of Paediatrics and Child Heath, Dr. Hiliary Cass, to review how clinical management and service provision for children and young people who are experiencing gender incongruence or gender-related distress can be improved.

33 'Senior child psychiatrist stood down after questioning gender medicine'; *The Australian*, Natasha Robinson, 15th June 2023.

Her observations in her interim report, published in 2022, included:

> *Aspects of the literature are open to interpretation in multiple ways, and there is a risk that some authors interpret their data from a particular ideological and/or theoretical standpoint.'*
>
> *The administration of puberty blockers is arguably more controversial than administration of the feminising/masculinising hormones, because there are more uncertainties associated with their use.'*
>
> *(T)he more contentious and important question is how fixed or fluid gender incongruence is at different ages and stages of development, and whether, regardless of aetiology, can be an inherent characteristic of the individual concerned. There is a spectrum of academic, clinical and societal opinion on this Having an open discussion about these questions is essential if a shared understanding of how to provide appropriate assessment and treatment is to be reached.*[34]

In June the National Health Service released a policy document which proposed that puberty blockers '*are "not routinely commissioned" as there is not enough evidence to support their safety or clinical effectiveness as a routinely available treatment and that they should only be accessed as part of research*'.[35]

34 *Independent review of gender identity services for children and young people: Interim report,* February, 2022.

35 *Consultation report for the interim service specification for specialist gender incongruence services for children and young people,* NHS England, 9th June 2023, p. 13.

These observations would appear to be consistent with Dr. Spencer's concerns. Yet columnists like *Crikey*'s Natalie Feliks continue to claim that '*transgender rights are a settled issue, agreed upon by medical experts and human rights commentators*'.[36]

Self-righteous radicals with a fascist mindset who pervade the transgender lobby share Ms. Feliks view. Within their ranks are those who believe that anybody who even acknowledges that there are divergent views within the medical profession is transphobic.

In November last year, *The New York Times* published a medical report on children who question their gender identity.[37] The results were mixed.

Commenting on the reaction to this report, Jonathon Chiat wrote in *The New York Magazine*:

> *The response on the left was as if the newspaper had committed a hate crime.*
>
> *This interpretation that the Times had contributed to an atmosphere of hatred against trans people was repeated so often and so stridently that within the left, it came to seem almost obvious.*
>
> *There is a familiar pattern here in the way left-wing activists shut down internal criticism by treating any criticism of their position as either identical to, or complicit with, the far right . If the*

36 'Read the room, politicians: no one wants your transgender rights culture war'. *Crikey*, 23rd June 2023

37 'They paused puberty but is there a cost?', *The New York Times,* 15th November 2022, Megan Twohey and Christina Jewett.

> *criticism is tempered and credible, this only makes them regard it as more dangerous.*
>
> *But this absolutist mind-set has had an especially pernicious effect on the issue of youth gender medicine. This is because the science is genuinely murky and embryonic.*[38]

Former US Secretary of State, Madeline Albright wrote that a fascist:

> *is someone who claims to speak for a whole nation or group, is utterly unconcerned with the rights of others, and is willing to use violence and whatever other means are necessary to achieve the goals he or she might have.*[39]

Ms. Albright also said that fascism is '*not an ideology, it's a process for gaining and keeping control.*'[40]

While the 'woke' brigade does not have any qualms about destroying the careers of people who disagree with them, it is not suggested that they are prepared to resort to violence. However, if the word 'violence' were deleted from Ms. Albright's definition, what would bc thc diffcrcncc bctwccn thcir typc of dictatorial behaviour and fascism?

38 'Helping Trans Kids Means Admitting What We Don't Know', *New York Magazine*, 15th December 2022.

39 *Fascism, A Warning* (Harper, New York, 2018).

40 *Madeline Albright on fascism, democracy and diplomacy*, Brookings, 11th September 2018.

Jean Jacques Rousseau

Jean Jacques Rousseau, the intellectual force underpinning the Enlightenment, is well-known for his influence on the French Revolution, but he also exerted considerable influence over America's founders and has had a significant influence on education theory.

Rousseau believed that '*man is born free, and he is everywhere in chains.*'[41] These chains are the external forces — civilisation, property, organised religion, family — which, he believes, corrupt humans:

> *The fundamental principle of all morality, upon which I have reasoned in all my writings and which I developed with all the clarity of which I am capable is that man is a being who is naturally good, loving justice and order; that there is no original perversity in the human heart, and the first movements of nature are always good.*[42]

For Rousseau feelings were pure because '*I had feelings before I had thoughts: that is the common lot of humanity*'.[43] Thus, he argued that feelings should determine our decisions and actions.

His legacy includes the notions of the primacy and inherent purity of the individual and the substitution of feelings for truth.

A challenge for those who consider themselves

41 *Du Contrat Social*, 1762.

42 *Rousseau and the Republic of Virtue: The Language of Politics in the French Revolution* (Cornell University 1986), Carol Blum, p. 103.

43 *The Confessions of Jean Jacques Rousseau*, Book 1.

classical liberals is that Rousseau's notion of self and his idea of the relationship between the individual and society have spawned ideas that he would not have envisaged. Liberalism has moved well beyond liberté, égalité, fraternité.

In the Anglo-Saxon world and, to varying degrees, the West, economic liberalism filled the ideological vacuum created by the demise of Marxism. Even before that, the futility of the 18th century liberals' social experiment using the family as a social tool had become evident. As Mr. Lasch pointed out:

> *The obligation to support a wife and children, in their view, would discipline possessive individualism. In the long run, of course, this attempt to build up the family as a counterweight to the acquisitive spirit was a lost cause.*[44]

This was an outcome which those who saw the family as one of Rousseau's chains welcomed. A self-described '*card-carrying member of the protest generation*' and founder of the Australia Institute, Dr. Clive Hamilton,

> *was convinced that the lifting of the suffocating constraints on sexual expression would be a source of liberation...*
>
> *We thought we were creating a new society and we knew our opponents were being defeated. The conservative establishment lost cause after cause...*[45]

As the social consequences of economic liberalism

44 'Conservatism Against Itself', *First Things*, April 1990.
45 *Can Porn Set Us Free?*, Speech to Sydney Writers Festival, 2003

have become undeniable, the influence of another manifestation of liberalism has become pervasive. An American historian Professor Carl Trueman explains in *The Rise and Triumph of the Modern Self*, gay marriage and transgenderism are not aspects of a new or original phenomenon. Rather they are the most recent symptoms of deep and long-established cultural pathologies in which the ideas of Rousseau play a prominent role.

Enter Antonio Gramsci

However, M. Rousseau's ideas have had assistance in their penetration of and ultimate domination of western, and particularly Anglo-Saxon, élites. That assistance has come from Antoni Gramsci, a founder of the Italian Communist Party and communism's greatest theoretician, who understood the power of ideas.

There are those who say that Marxism or socialism lost the fight but won the war. It would be more accurate to say that Karl Marx lost the fight, but Antonio Gramsci won the war. Sig. Gramsci saw that a revolution based on economic determinism would not succeed outside Russia:

> *In Russia the State was everything, civil society was primordial and gelatinous; in the West, there was a proper relation between State and civil society, and when the State trembled a sturdy structure of*

> *civil society was at once revealed.*[46]

He was amongst the first to understand that, to use the words of an American communist and editor of *Theoretical Review* Paul Saba:

> *Bolshevism failed to understand that the oppression of multi-class social groupings such as women, national minorities and Jews, was rooted in society relatively independently of class oppression, and was therefore reproduced by a multiplicity of political, ideological, national and cultural factors, as well as economic-class relations.*[47]

Thus, in the words of the editor of an English edition of *Prison Notebooks*, the late Joseph Buttigieg,

> *one should refrain from facile rhetoric about direct attacks against the State (which Sig. Gramsci termed "a war of manoeuvre") and concentrate instead on the difficult and immensely complicated tasks that a 'war of position' within civil society entails.*[48]

The 'war on position', which now is described as cultural hegemony, is an intellectual and cultural war designed to gain control of what *Spectator* columnist Henry Fairlie called 'The Establishment' in 1955.

Thus, the culture of today's élites in the West, and

46 *Selections from the Prison Notebooks* (International Publishers, New York, 1971), p.238.

47 'Antonio Gramsci and the Recasting of Marxist Strategy'. Theoretical Review No. 25, November-December 1981.

48 'The Contemporary Discourse on Civil Society', *Boundary 2*, Spring 2005, p.41.

Anglo-Saxon countries in particular, is testament to the brilliance of Sig. Gramsci and the role his strategy has played in infesting ideas which can be traced to the foundations of Rosseau.

A Tale of Two Cultures

However, the domination of liberalism as the philosophy of inner metropolitan élites, who believe that they have total control over their lives and lifestyles, is not replicated in the value systems of residents in the outer suburbs and regions.[49]

There life marches to the beat of a different drum. Few, if any residents, have heard of the person considered to be the founder of conservatism, Edmund Burke, but, of necessity, their values and lifestyles reflect conservative values. If they were asked if they supported these Burkean sentiments:

> *To be attached to the subdivision, to love the little platoon we belong to in society, is the first principle (the germ as it were) of public affections. It is the first link in the series by which we proceed towards a love to our country, and to mankind...*
>
> *We begin our public affections in our families. No cold relation is a zealous citizen. We pass on to our neighbourhoods, and our habitual provincial connexions';* and

49 For an analysis of the gulf between the inner metropolitan suburbs and the outer suburbs and regions, see *A Tale of Two Cities*, https://philosophymatters.substack.com/p/a-tale-of-two-nations.

> *Society 'becomes a partnership not only between those who are living, but between those who are living, those who are dead, and those who are to be born,*[50] many would agree.

It is apparent that, for the élites, however they have been constituted through the ages, 'democracy' has been useful only while the masses tolerated or accepted their priorities, interests and beliefs or when the divergence of interests was camouflaged, whether intentionally or otherwise.

The Power of One — or a Few

As resistance to the arrogance of the élites and their by-passing of democratic structures has been increasing, their determination to maintain their power and control is being exposed.

That resistance has intensified. It is not just the political pushback in Europe.

Last year and this year, a few professional sports players unknowingly emulated an obscure member of the US Congress in the 1980s, Charlie Wilson who, arguably, single-handedly oversaw the defeat of the Soviet Union in Afghanistan by organising the arming and equipping of the mujāhidūn, thereby demonstrating the power of one.

In Australia last year, a National Rugby League (NRL)

---

50 *Reflections on the Revolution in France,* 1790. Paragraphs 75, 331 and 165 respectively.

team, Manly, became the first NRL team to decide to wear Pride jerseys for one round. Seven players refused, because they believed that doing so would conflict with their religious beliefs and they stood down for that round. The team lost an important game and the saga split the club which failed to play finals.

There had been suggestions that National Rugby League teams would play a Pride round this year. Nothing has eventuated. In an annual survey of coaches and assistant coaches in January, the coaches were evenly divided on whether they would encourage players to wear a Pride jersey and only a third of coaches supported the idea of a Pride round.[51]

The decision of National Rugby League stands in stark contrast to the Australian Football League (AFL) (Australian rules) which has been captured by the 'woke' agenda as has been demonstrated by Hawthorn's and the AFL's handling of unsubstantiated allegations by Aboriginal players, and Essendon's sacking last year of a CEO it appointed 24 hours before because he is a member of a church which opposes gay marriage.

Earlier this year, seven ice hockey players from six teams in Canada and the USA refused to wear Pride jerseys because they believe that doing so conflicts with their religious beliefs. Seven teams also did not wear Pride jerseys.

Some of players are Russian and at least one a

51 'NRL coaches survey results', David Riccio, Brent Read and others, *Daily Telegraph*, 2nd February, 2023.

member of the Russian Orthodox Church. Two teams said that they had acted to protect their players, laying responsibility for their decisions at the feet of Russian President Vladimir Putin. Last December the Russian parliament passed a law further restricting the promotion of 'non-traditional sexual relations' in film, online, advertising or in public. Individuals and organisation can be fined substantial sums of money for '*propagandising nontraditional sexual relations*'. The patriarch of the Russian Orthodox Church is a strong supporter of the legislation.

However, that explanation fell flat after the Deputy Commissioner of the National Hockey League, Bill Daly, said that the NHL did not have any information to suggest that its Russian players are facing 'material' threats, either in Russia or elsewhere, if they choose to participate in teams' Pride night activities.[52]

Also, as Canadian hockey writer Ian Kennedy pointed out, several players who refused to wear Pride jerseys were not Russian[53] and at least six Russian players did wear Pride jerseys.

Columnist Scott Stinson wrote:

> *It doesn't take much research to discover that punishment for violating the law is just a fine, that enforcement is rare, and that there was never any indication that Russia was going to try to apply it*

52 'NHL: Nothing to suggest Russian players at risk for participating in Pride nights', Scott Powers, *The Athletic*, 26th March, 2023.

53 'Why are NHL players refusing to wear Pride jerseys? Explaining the league's latest controversy', *Yahoo Sports Canada*. 5th April, 2023.

> *beyond its own borders. Do Russian NHL players honestly think that someone back home is going to come after them for wearing a small rainbow patch on their jersey for 20 minutes while they do a few laps around the ice with their teammates?*[54]

The first player to refuse to wear a Pride jersey was Philadelphia Flyers' defenseman Ivan Provorov. After the announcement, his jerseys were the number one jersey trending and were sold out on NHL Shop.com and NHL Fanatics.com.[55]

When Mr. Provorov made his decision in January the National Hockey League did not appear to be concerned. Commissioner Gary Bettman said:

> *(I)ndividual players are gonna make their decisions and follow their beliefs. Having said that, when you look at all of our players and the commitments that they've made to social causes and to making our game inclusive, let's focus on the 700 that embrace it and not one or two that may have some issues for their own personal reasons.*[56]

By the end of March, Mr. Bettman was signalling that the backlash was something that the NHL '*will have to evaluate in the offseason*':

> *I think that's become more of a distraction now, because the substance of what our teams and we*

54 'NHL's Pride Nights were to send a message of inclusivity. They are doing the opposite', *National Post,* 24th March 2023.
55 'NHL Commissioner Gary Bettman Defends Ivan Provorov in Recent Statement', *Flyers Insider,* S. Harper, 4th February 2023.
56 'Gary Bettman stands by NHL's diversity effort despite Ivan Provorov incident', *New York Post*, Ethan Sears, 19th January 2023.

> *have been doing and stand for is really being pushed to the side for what is a handful of players basically have made personal decisions, and you have to respect that as well.*[57]

In June the Board of Governors decided that from next season teams will not wear themed jerseys because they have '*become a distraction and taking away from the fact that all of our clubs in some form or another host nights in honour of various groups or causes.*'[58]

Meanwhile, trouble was brewing on the baseball front. Last year, three major league baseball teams, the Tampa Bay Raiders, the San Francisco Giants and the Los Angeles Dodgers, decided to put Pride logos on their uniforms. At least five Raiders' players removed the logos.

This year, the Los Angeles Dodgers awarded their Community Hero Award to the Sisters of the Perpetual Indulgence, a group of men who dress in nuns' habits and ridicule and parody the Roman Catholic Church, and invited them to their Pride Night. The decision sparked protests from a range of people including Senator Marco Rubio and the President of the Catholic League for Religious and Civil Rights and the Dodgers withdrew the invitation.

Following that decision, a threat by gay and lesbian

---

57 NHL's Gary Bettman suggests league will reevaluate Pride-themed jersey nights amid spate of opt-outs', *Fox News,* Ryan Gaydos, 29th March 2023.

58 'NHL doing away with Pride jerseys, other speciality uniforms in warmups', *Sportsnet,* 22nd June 2023.

organisations and the American Civil Liberties Union of South California to boycott the night resulted in a renewal of the invitation.

That decision led to a statement by the United States Conference of Catholic Bishops condemning it and describing it as blasphemy and the Archbishop of San Francisco, Salvatore Cordileone tweeted:

> *Our Catholic sisters devote themselves to serving others selflessly. Decent people would not mock & blaspheme them. So we now know what gods the Dodger admin worships. Open desecration & anti-Catholicism is not disqualifying. Disappointing but not surprising. Gird your loins.*[59]

Two players from the team publicly disagreed with the decision, as did Trevor Williams from the Washington Nationals, who encouraged '*my fellow Catholics to reconsider their support of an organisation that allows this type of mockery of its fans to occur.*'[60]

There was a protest on the night of the game. A march of about 2,000 people before the game forced the closure of the stadium's main entrance. Meanwhile, in a relatively empty stadium inside, the award was being presented.

It is only two years since MLB moved the 2021 All-Star Game from Atlanta to Denver as protest over changes to Georgia's voting laws. However, on the 16th June the

---

59 Twitter, Archbishop Salvatore J. Cordileone@ArchCordileone, 23rd May 2023.

60 Twitter, Trevor Williams@MeLLamoTrevor, 31st May 2023.

MLB commissioner Rob Manfred said that:

> *We have told teams, in terms of actual uniforms, hats, bases that we don't think putting logos on them is a good idea just because of the desire to protect players: not putting them in a position of doing something that may make them uncomfortable because of their personal views.*[61]

Consumer Power

At the same time, the masses experienced what minority cultural groups have understood for years — consumer power, which like social power, is more influential than political power.

For example, LGBT Capital, a U.K.-based investment company, estimates the USA has more than 17 million LGBTQ+ people with more than $1 trillion in spending power[62] — a sword it wields with great effect.

In March, a transgender woman and influencer for what was the USA's then best-selling beer Bud Light, uploaded a post on Instagram showing a can of beer with her face on it specially made to celebrate her first year as a woman. There was an immediate backlash.

Sales of Bud Light plummeted and by July it was number 14 on the list of the USA's most popular beers.

61 Twitter, Chelsea Janes, Washington Post, 16th June 2023.
62 'Pride becomes a minefield for big companies, but many continue their support', Anne D. Innocenzio and Dee-Ann Durbin, *Associated Press*, New York, 5th June 2023.

Since April the share price of Anheuser Busch InBev has fallen by 20 per cent.

In May, American retail giant Target displayed LGBT-themed children's merchandise, including a baby bodysuit with both Pride and transgender flags.

Following a consumer backlash, Target either removed or relocated the clothing in a number of stores, and particularly Southern stores. Target attributed its move to protestor behaviour. By the middle of July Target's share price had fallen from US$161 to US$130.

Follow the Money

These incidents are a demonstration of what is called 'stakeholder capitalism', the driving force behind which is the World Economic Forum, an organisation with one member — its Founder and Chairman Professor Klaus Schwab.

A former President of Anheuser-Busch Sales and Distribution Co Anson Frericks has explained what stakeholder capitalism is, how it has been implemented and how three investment funds, which together manage US$20 trillion, are the drivers of 'woke' corporate governance. He says:

> *(T)he USA's greatest enterprises have been repurposed into vehicles of social change*
>
> *BlackRock, State Street and Vanguard (are) the three largest and most influential financial*

> *institutions in U.S. history. Together, the Big Three constitute the largest shareholders of nearly 90 per cent of the largest companies listed on the U.S. stock exchange.*
>
> *The Big Three are proponents of what's called 'stakeholder capitalism'.*
>
> *2019 was a turning point.*
>
> *That year a group of CEOs from America's largest companies, adopted a new Statement on the Purpose of a Corporation declaring that all companies 'share a fundamental commitment to all of our stakeholders' to promote the larger social good.*[63]

Two years prior to that BlackRock Chairman and CEO Larry Fink had said at a New York Times DealBook Summit:

> *The behavior is going to have to change this is something we're asking companies. You have to force behavior. At BlackRock, we are forcing behaviors.*[64]

Mr. Frericks believes that business has been:

> *paralyzed by corporate America's forced adoption of 'stakeholder' capitalism, which preaches to companies about why they must serve activists,*

---

63 'How your 401k savings are being used to turn our biggest brands woke as revealed by ex-Anheuser-Busch exec who shows how you can fight back at the cash registers', *Daily Mail*, 29th May 2023.

64 'Video Emerges of BlackRock CEO gloating about Using Woke Ideology to Force Behaviors of Public', Frank Bergan, *Slay* 7th June 2023.

> *politicians, non-governmental organizations and all manner of interests – anyone really apart from their shareholders and customers!*[65]

Klaus Schwab

From the 1970s the mantra in business was 'shareholder capitalism' which was a manifestation of Milton Friedman's liberalism and based on his doctrine that:

> *There is one and only one social responsibility of business – to use its resources and engage in activities designed to increase its profits so long as it engages in open and free competition without deception or fraud.*[66]

With the collapse of communism, the economic liberals were triumphalist. From around 2010 the social consequences of this mantra and the widening wealth gap which have flowed from economic rationalism have been undeniable and increasingly have become politically unsustainable.

Enter Klaus Schwab who has been biding his time for 50 years. He saw the demise of Mr. Friedman's doctrine as an opportunity '*to ensure that stakeholder capitalism remains the new dominant model.*'[67] He first described this

---

65 'Anheuser-Busch's CEO has failed to fix the Bud Light crisis. He must quit NOW and let someone else right this sinking ship... for the sake of ordinary Americans' 401(k)s', *Daily Mail,* 1st July 2022.

66 'A Friedman doctrine The Social Responsibility is to Increase Profits', *The New York Times Magazine,* 13th September 1970.

67 *Why we need the 'Davos Manifesto' for a better kind of capitalism*, World Economic Forum, 1st December 2019.

concept which positions '*private corporations as trustees of society*' in 1971 and he '*created the World Economic Forum to help business and political leaders implement it*'.[68]

In 2020 the World Economic Forum adopted stakeholder capitalism. By then, the International Business Council, which includes Deloitte, Ernst & Young, PriceWaterhouseCooper and KPMG, had signed up to the concept of environmental, social and governance (ESG) goals.

The outcome has resulted in an alliance between the financial and social élites. With the élites' ability to exercise their power and control from the shadows having become more circumscribed, this outcome has meant that the control and influence that the élites exert over society, including 'democratic' societies, has become even more apparent.

Economic Fascism?

The response of Mark Hornshaw, a lecturer at Notre Dame University Australia to the adoption of shareholder capitalism is that:

> *A system that replaces the goals of true stakeholders with the iron will of ruling elites, which retains nominal private ownership, but uses government force to pressure firms to serve centrally determined goals, looks and smells an awful lot like economic fascism.*[69]

68 *Why we need the 'Davos Manifesto' for a better kind of capitalism*
69 *Is Stakeholder Capitalism' Newspeak for Economic fascism,* Foundation for Economic Education, 23rd January 2021.

Reporter Salena Zito, co-author of *The Great Revolt: Inside the Populist Coalition Reshaping American Politics* has highlighted that the decisions of the Big Three demonstrate that:

> *Rarely today are owners of national brands a "local" man or woman who built it from the ground up. Instead, companies tend to be owned by funds and conglomerates with boards of directors who live in coastal centers of wealth and power. And the worldview of these owners is disconnected from the people who buy their products.*[70]

A good example is Marc Benioff, Founder and CEO of Salesforce, a cloud computing company. When asked in 2016:

> *Lawmakers, politicians – they're held accountable to the public when they are not seen as doing something for the public good. Doesn't that make it dangerous for companies and CEOs to be doing stuff like this because who are you accountable to?*

He replied,

> *I think that's old thinking, honestly. I am quite accountable to many different stakeholders, including my shareholders, my large investors, to my board of directors, to my employees, to my customers, to my partners, to the communities that I live. I live in a city called San Francisco. And it is very much a city that is activist oriented. And I'll tell you, in our city, people hold you accountable*

---

70 'Target and Bud Light are hurting, but Mark Cuban says wokeness is good business', *Pittsburgh Post-Gazette*, 11th June 2023.

> *for doing the right thing.*

When asked:

> *for people who say they're worried that they have people from the business world who are sort of helping to lead these debates instead of policymakers and politicians who were actually voted in by the public, I mean, how do you respond to that?*

He replied,

> *because our government leaders tend to be a little weaker than they were, CEOs have to step up and be a little stronger and have a bigger voice, which is what exactly is happening in these states.*

Mr. Benioff also said that he got involved in issues about which '*I really don't know that much about to be honest with you.*'[71]

These incidents are practical examples of Mr. Lasch's 'alternative' institutions created by the élites and of the chasm between the élites' views and those of the rest of us.

A Turning of the Tide?

Brad Todd, a Republican strategist and the other co-author of *The Great Revolt*, thinks that until there is more cultural diversity in the boardroom, control of the media, educational organizations, high tech

71 'CEO Uses Company's Clout to Get Involved In Controversial State Measures', *National Public Radio,* 23rd May 2016.

companies, financial institutions and entertainment businesses will remain disconnected.[72]

Events such as Brexit, the ongoing support for the Le Pens in France and political uncertainty in Europe generally, the rise of Donald Trump and the latest furore involving Nigel Farage are the political fallout from the consequences of stakeholder capitalism which ignores the interests of the masses in the outer suburbs and the regions and their equivalents.

Time will tell if Mr. Todd is right and stakeholder capitalism is generating '*a polarization that will continue to sort and impact our politics.*' There are some indications that he is right. Pallavi Gogoi, Chief Business Editor of National Public Radio wrote in June:

> *In the last 10 years or so, some corporations have gone further, advocating for marriage equality and publicly pushing for anti-discrimination laws.*
>
> *That activism has played a big role in "how American society views queer people, their relationships, and their families," says Carlos A. Ball, Rutgers law professor, in his book* The Queering of Corporate America.
>
> *All of that may be at stake now, as corporations face immense pressure – including threats to life and property and being jeered as "woke"– for supporting LGBTQ causes.*
>
> *Very, very powerful companies ... are being essentially silenced or feeling cowed by, or politically*

72 'Target and Bud Light are hurting'.

intimidated, by the ferocious right wing backlash against LGBTQ gains.[73]

Further, Forbes Media chairman Steve Forbes has put a public spotlight on consumer power:

I think in terms of the whole marketing thing.

The consumer is ultimately the ruler and that's what these companies have to keep in mind.

'If you are not performing, your stock takes a hit, shareholders get uneasy. You are going be out of a job if you're CEO.

The market ultimately works, and the market is people.[74]

Reporter Tony Owusu reflected Mr. Forbes observation:

The real victory has been the right's ability to change Budweiser and Target's behavior.

The right has made it its mission to force corporations out of the political discussion.

With their campaigns against Bud Light and Target they are close to achieving that goal as corporations begin to weigh the cost of their political decisions.

At least for now.

This is the true victory of the right's boycott

---

73 'How the Bud Light boycott shows brands at a crossroads: Use their voice, or shut up?', *National Public Radio*, 28th June 2023.

74 *The Bottom Line,* Fox Business Network, 12th April 2023.

campaign.[75]

Tim Knavish, CEO of PPG Industries, a paint manufacturer is an example.

> *We run a business. We don't run a political organization. We don't run a religious organization, and we don't run a social organization.*
>
> *However, [we] recognize that we operate in a society. We hire employees with opinions and views. We work with customers that have opinions and views. So we have to take all that into account.*[76]

The Advertising Industry's Take on Events

This sentiment is also finding expression elsewhere.

The Cannes Lions International Festival of Creativity bestows the world's most prestigious advertising awards. This year the focus of the awards changed. According to one juror, jurors '*should remember that what we do can be entertaining, can be inspiring, and it's for brands selling shit*'. According to co-founder of *Semafor* and former *New York Times* columnist Ben Smith '*that juror and four other people familiar with the messaging said it focused on celebrating light-hearted, lucrative advertising over heavier, more political content.*'[77]

---

75 'While the Right Celebrates Wins Over Bud Light, Target, They're Cheering the Wrong Victory', *The Street,* 12th June 2023.

76 'Companies That Embraced Social Issues Have Second Thoughts', Chip Cutter and Lauren Weber, *Wall Street Journal*, 7th June 2023.

77 'Dial Down the Politics, Cannes Lions ad festival tells jurors', 20th June, *Semafor Media,* 2023.

Mr. Smith wrote that '*the push to extract corporations from politics is part of the same global trend away from the social-media driven progressive movements that dominated the 2010s.*' That began in earnest in earnest in 2022 when chief brand officer at Procter and Gamble, Marc Pritchard said advertising had '*gone too far into the good" at the expense of commercial goals*'.

The use by minorities to use financial clout and purchasing power strategically always has had a weakness. Its effectiveness has depended on the rest of the market's not engaging in similar tactics. In the cases of Anheuser-Busch and Target that assumption proved erroneous. Both companies are paying the price and they, and others, are considering the long-term effects.

Oxygen Financial CEO Ted Jenkin sums up the issue when the bluff is called and the majority of customers vote strategically:

> *Why in the world would you go after 1 per cent, less than 1 per cent of our country that are transgender and think that that's going to make an influence on getting more young people to drink Bud Light?*[78]

Time will tell if these events represent a hiccup for the élites, which can be negated by beating a tactical retreat to the shadows, or whether they are a harbinger of a broader revolt by the masses. A problem for the élites is that their implementation of stakeholder

78 'Bud Light's Dylan Mulvaney problem won't cripple Anheuser-Busch, but will tarnish reputation, experts Say', *Fox News,* Brian Flood, David Ritz, 14th April 2023.

capitalism seems to require a brutal exercise of power that reasonably could be described as fascist.

Davos Man

What we do know is that management will not be easily deterred from performing their self-appointed '*role of a trustee of the material universe for future generations*'[79]. We also know that the chasm between the élites and the masses in views and interests is long-standing and deep-seated. In 2004 the late Professor Samuel Huntington wrote that '*the central distinction between the public and elites is not isolationism versus internationalism, but nationalism versus cosmopolitanism*'.[80]

He also contended that '*the pervasive and fundamental forces of economic globalization make it likely that the denationalizing of elites will continue*' and drew attention to Adam Smith's observation that:

> *The proprietor of land is necessarily a citizen of the particular country in which his estate lies. The proprietor of stock is properly a citizen of the world, and is not necessarily attached to any particular country.*[81]

Mr. Huntington postulated that:

> *The involvement of individuals in globalizing*

79 *Davos Manifesto 1973: A Code of Ethics for Business leaders.*

80 'Dead Souls: the Denationalization of the American Elites', *The National Interest*, 1st March 2004.

81 *Wealth of Nations,* Book V, Part II, Article II.

> *processes varies almost directly with their socio-economic status. Elites have more and deeper transnational interests, commitments and identities.*

Mr. Huntington popularised the term 'Davos man' to describe '*a new global elite*':

> *Estimated to number about 20 million in 2000, of whom 40 percent were American, this elite is expected to double in size by 2010. Comprising fewer than 4 percent of the American people, these transnationalists have little need for national loyalty, view national boundaries as obstacles that thankfully are vanishing, and see national governments as residues from the past whose only useful function is to facilitate the elite's global operations. In the coming years, one corporation executive confidently predicted,* "the only people who will care about national boundaries are politicians."

That today's Davos Man and Woman are, as Mr. Huntington pointed out, the antithesis of their business predecessors, is a testament to the power of ideas. Mr. Schwab has been harbouring for 50 years an idea which dates back to the 1930s. A comparison can be made between the glitterati of the transnational business, political activist and NGO sets who frequent Davos every January and Charles Wilson, the President of General Motors, who President Eisenhower nominated as Secretary of Defense in 1953. In Mr. Wilson's confirmation hearings before the Senate Armed Services Committee he said that:

> *for years I thought that what was good for our*

country was good for General Motors and vice versa.

Our company is too big. It goes with the welfare of the country.[82]

A Metaphor

Earlier this year the Coutts Bank told British TV presenter and leader of the Brexit campaign, Nigel Farage, who had been a customer of the bank for more than 40 years, that they intended to close his accounts. A reason for the decision was not provided.

Mr. Farage then unsuccessfully sought to open a bank account with numerous banks. At the end of June, the bank closed his account. Mr. Farage said that other members of his family also had experienced difficulties with opening or maintaining bank accounts.

Mr. Farage publicised his experience, tweeting that:

I have been given no explanation or recourse as to why this is happening to me. This is serious political persecution at the very highest level of our system. If they can do it to me, they can do it to you too.[83]

In response, Dame Alison Rose, the CEO of the NatWest Bank (the new name for the discredited Royal Bank of Scotland which was salvaged by British taxpayers in 2008 during the financial crisis) which

82 Transcript of hearings before the Senate Committee on Armed Services, 15th January, 1953, p. 26.

83 @Nigel_Farage, Twitter, 29th June 2023.

is the parent company of the Coutts Bank, told the BBC's business editor Simon Jack[84] that the account was being closed because Mr. Farage did not meet the financial criteria for having an account with Coutts – a private bank, which means that it is an exclusive bank for the wealthy.

Mr. Jack subsequently thanked:

> *Coutts customers who have been in touch saying they fall below financial thresholds but unlike Farage have not been threatened with account closure. Clearly a lot of discretion available to the bank.*[85]

Mr. Farage obtained the dossier Coutts had prepared on him which revealed a 40-page report which said:

- Mr. Farage's economic contribution was '*now sufficient to retain on a commercial basis*'.
- Mr. Farage's engagement with it is what it expected — professional, polite and respectful.
- Mr. Farage had not made any inappropriate remarks to staff and treated them professionally and with courtesy.
- There is no evidence of direct links with Russia.
- Although no legal or other censure had occurred, it is clear that Mr. Farage's views on climate change and race do not align with

84 @BBCSimonJack, Twitter, 4th July 2023.
85 @BBCSimonJack, Twitter, 5th July 2023.

its purposes.

- Mr. Farage comments and articles about ESG, Diversity and Inclusion are not in line with its views or its purpose.
- Mr. Farage at best is seen as xenophobic and pandering to racists, and at worst is seen as xenophobic and racist.
- Many of the behaviours demonstrated by Nigel Farage do not align with Coutts' values and that there are reputational risks to the bank in being associated with him
- Continuing to bank Nigel Farage was not compatible with Coutts given his publicly-stated views that were at odds with its position as an inclusive organisation.

> *Under Rose, NatWest and Coutts promoted an agenda around the idea of 'purpose', which included climate change, sustainable living and LGBTQ+ rights.*[86]

The Spectator described:

> *NatWest's attack on Farage as a political hit-job, but the board of NatWest, which owns Coutts, seem to have thought their actions were reasonable. Their main regret seems to be not that all this happened, but that it became public.*[87]

86 'Nigel Farge, NatWest and the fight over 'woke' capitalism', *Financial Times*, 29th July 2023, Jim Pickard and Stephen Morris.

87 *The Spectator*, 29th July 2023.

It said that the Farage affair:

> *can be traced back to the day, two years ago, when the bank proudly announced that it had achieved 'B Corp' status. B Corp's website declares: "Certified B Corporations are leaders in the global movement for an inclusive, equitable and regenerative economy." It adds that its scheme seeks to measure 'a company's entire social and environmental impact'.*

Dame Alison was, but no longer is, a member of the Government's business council, the Government's energy efficiency taskforce and the net zero council. Like counterparts in Australia, she stopped new loans to oil and gas companies, another decision which highlights the gulf between the views of the élites and those of the masses. The Conservative Party government, as the largest shareholder acquiesced in this decision, but recently it has decided to issue new licences for oil and gas drilling in the North Sea. Presumably it is happy for this drilling to be financed by overseas banks. Tellingly, on the government's decision to issue new drilling licences, a You Gov poll of 3295 British adults conducted on the 31st July revealed that 42 per cent thought the decision was right, 27 per cent thought it was wrong and 31 per cent did not know.

This puts a spotlight on the chair the NatWest board Howard Davies. Mr. Farage said:

> *Howard Davies, who of course describes himself as the chairperson of the NatWest Group, it was he that put*

> *Alison Rose in place, it was the board that sanctioned this culture.*
>
> *A culture that talks about diversity and inclusion.*[88]

Mr. Farage's opinion is supported by the thoughts of a top 20 investor that '*the board must have known the reason for his being excluded from Coutts.*'[89]

Sir Howard Davies was appointed by a Conservative Party government in 2015. Were Mr. Fairlie still alive, he no doubt would say that Mr. Davies is eminently appropriate to hold such a position. After all, he is an Oxford man. However, journalist Stephen Pollard[90] suggests that his career has been chequered, one example being his support during the 1990s for the United Kingdom's disastrous decision to join the Exchange Rate Mechanism.

However, a more memorable event in his career is the reason for his departure as the director of the London School of Economics in 2011. Sir Howard, who seemingly is not fussed about overseeing a process which concluded that Mr. Farage's being a customer constituted a reputational risk, was equally not fussed about the LSE's soliciting a £1.5 million donation from Libyan dictator Colonel Gaddafi's foundation and

88 'Nigel Farage demands entire NatWest board quits after it attempted to keep Alison Rose in job', *GB News' Breakfast with Eammon and Isabel,* 26th July 2023.

89 'NatWest fails to stem Farage pressure as shareholders turn against board', *Financial Times,* Harriet Agnew, Stephen Morris and Jim Pichard, 27th July 2023.

90 'The breathtaking arrogance of NatWest chairman and serial failure of Sir Howard Davies', *Daily Mail,* 28th July 2023.

securing a signing of a £2.2 million contract to train Libyan officials.

Mr. Farage's story has it all:

- the Establishment's appointing as Chair of the board of the bank, someone who Sir Humphrey Appleby of *Yes Minister* fame would describe as 'reliable',
- a prime example of stakeholder capitalism in action,
- the gulf in views between the élites and the masses (Mr Farage said that '*the upper middle class, wealthy London metropolitan ŭlite*' would no doubt support the assessment of Coutts' Bank[91]), and,
- the self-righteous, dictatorial mindset of the élites.

However, it does not end there. As the good ship NatWest began to take on water, it was allowed to drift by itself. Both the Prime Minister and Labour's leader swum away as fast as they could. Prime Minister Rishi Sunak said:

> *What I said right at the start of this was that it wasn't right for people to be deprived of basic services like banking because of their views.*
>
> *This isn't about any one individual, it's about values – do you believe in free speech and not to be discriminated against because of your legally*

91 Twitter, 29th June 2023.

held views?[92]

Labor leader Sir Keir Starmer told BBC Radio 5 5 Live:

> *I certainly don't think anybody should be refused banking services because of their political views, whoever they are.*

This sentiment was echoed by Anthony Quigley, a co-founder of the Corporate Governance Institute. who argued that '*ESG should not be confused with the radical 'woke' brigade*' and that Mr. Farage's '*freedom of speech matters just as much as anyone else's.*'[93] However, the ESG industry is the instrument for enforcing the 'woke' agenda, as a former President of Anheuser-Busch Sales and Distribution Co Anson Frericks has pointed out and the existence of an organisation called B Lab which certifies companies as 'B Corp' demonstrates.

In political circles especially, it is fashionable to think that liberalism, individualism and progressivism are all different. However, they all have the same philosophic foundations, which can have consequences which cause discomfort. As American historian Professor Carl Trueman has highlighted, the problem for Mr. Sunak, Mr. Quigley and for people who consider themselves classic liberals, is the fact that freedom of speech's now being seen as a problem rather than a solution is a manifestation of the latest form of individualism or liberalism which has gained the cultural ascendancy.

---

92 *Sky News*, 27th July 2023.

93 'Farage calls diversity and inclusion culture 'divisive' as governance row erupts'. *Evening Standard*, Rebecca Speare-Cole, 27th July 2023.

He observes that:

> *The notion of assault on the person becomes not simply — or even primarily — a matter that involves damage to the body or to property. It becomes psychological. (F)reedom of speech becomes not so much part of the solution as part of the problem.*[94]

There is something else that the Conservative Party and its equivalents in other countries do not understand. Tim Montgomerie, a former adviser to Boris Johnson notes that many Tories genuinely share Farage's:

> *genuine moral disdain for the woke agenda... Milton Friedman said that chocolate companies should make chocolate and make money for their shareholders . . . Companies should stick to their core remit.*[95]

The challenge for the self-professed champions of free markets, like the Conservative Party and its equivalents, is that many of them have sat on their hands while the transnational, financial élite, at the urging of Klaus Schwab, have ditched Milton Friedman's shareholder capitalism, adopted stakeholder capitalism and, as demonstrated by NatWest, are implementing it with a ruthlessness articulated by BlackRock's Larry Finks.

Representatives of the 'woke' governance industry have taken different paths. Michael Evans, a former head of communications at Baker McKenzie in London

94 *The Rise and Triumph of the Modern Self Crossway*, Wheaton, Illinois, 2020), p. 326.

95 'Nigel Farage, NatWest and the fight over 'woke' capitalism', *Financial Times,* Jim Pickard and Stephen Morris, 29th July 2023.

and now a director at a litigation and reputation consultancy, echoed Mr. Quigley's sentiments and said that:

> *a risk-based decision about a politically exposed person had nothing at all to do with ESG and corporate values In dropping Farage as a client, this was an example of virtue signalling gone too far by Coutts.*[96]

Justin Doherty, chairman of reputation risk advisers Hemington Consulting went further saying Natwest:

> *shows what happens when a company or institution goes rogue and – in the most hypocritical manner imaginable – uses the cloak of ESG and ethics to behave badly.*
>
> *It is a tragedy that well-intentioned initiatives such as diversity and inclusion and ESG have been subverted in this way, and hijacked by narrow agendas and partisan interests.*[97]

Attempting to explain away NatWest's decision away as 'going rogue' and distancing ESG from 'woke' defies the pub test. Mr. Frericks has explained who drives 'woke' governance and how it works and the now former CEO, Dame Alison did not have a reputation for taking risks.

NatWest is not the only corporation chasing B Corp

---

96 'What does Farage v Coutts row mean for ESG', *The Times,* Jonathon Ames, 27th July 2023.

97 'Farage calls diversity and inclusion culture 'divisive' as governance row erupts'.

status, or flaunting its support of Pride week. Nor is it the only financial institution accused of 'woke' governance. A couple of days before the Farage bombshell exploded, another of the big four banks, Barclays Bank, while denying liability, paid more than £20,000 to settle a discrimination claim launched by the Core Issues Trust and the International Federation for Therapeutic and Counselling Choice. The Trust supports men and women who voluntarily seek to change their sexual preference, expression or gender identity. In 2020, the Bank, which is ranked by Stonewall as a top-ranked LGBT employer, suspended the charity's accounts. The charity said that Barclay's responded to pressure from LGBT campaigners.[98]

Since Mr. Farage announced his situation, an Anglican minister, Richard Fothergill, has revealed that the Yorkshire Building Society decided to close his account after he responded to a monthly email from the bank asking for feedback. He objected to the Bank's promotion of transgender ideology during Pride month.

In what seems similar to Mr. Farage's experience, the Bank advised him four days' later that his account would be closed because their relationship had '*irrevocably broken down*' and that it had a '*zero tolerance approach to discrimination*'.[99]

98 'Barclays Bank pay out £20k for closing Christian account', *The Times*, James Beal, 28th June 2023.

99 'Yorkshire Building Society 'closed vicar's account after trans protest', *The Times*, James Beal, 1st July 2023.

In what may have seemed like comic relief for Mr. Farage while he was preoccupied with sorting out of his finances in the last week of June, another issue emerged.

This year the Television and Radio Industries Club changed the voting system for its awards and let the public be the judges. As a nominee for an award, Mr. Farage attended the gala awards' night. In a forerunner of what was to come, he tweeted that he was asked to leave the drinks area of the main sponsor. Subsequently he was invited back.

The media élite was later shocked when it was announced that he won the award for best news presenter and heckled and booed him. He thanked '*all those good, ordinary folk who live outside the M25 for voting for me*' — another reminder of the cultural divide between the British equivalent of the inner suburbs and the outer suburbs and regions.

What is to be done?

For those who reject the priorities, beliefs, values and the cultural tyranny of the élites the question, made famous by Vladimir Lenin is: What is to be done?

Even if the power and influence historically exerted by the élites were diminished, it would not reduce the cultural gulf between them and the masses which has emerged with the tumbling down of the Berlin wall in 1989 and the triumphal declaration of victory by economic liberals.

The élites always have been with us. The cultural revolutionaries of the 1960s taking "Liberté, égalité, fraternité" literally and thinking that those ideals would be the new foundations of society were naïve.

Rousseau's influence and that of his successors has been apparent since the American Revolution and, courtesy of Sig. Gramsci's strategy, now it has become entrenched. The consequences of this evolution have been compounded by the ascendancy of stakeholder capitalism under which the élites exercise what they consider to be their right to enforce on the masses how to act and how to think.

The mindset and beliefs of today's élites is different from what it was prior to the triumphalism of economic liberalism after the Berlin Wall came down. Prior to the 1990s, within them there was a sense of 'noblesse oblige'. Mr. Wilson's resigning as the President of General Motors to become the Secretary for Defense reflects this mindset.

This concept was resented because it reinforced class status and was considered to demean the masses and reflect a sense of the superiority of the élites. However, what it also did was reflect a sense of obligation, limited though that may have been, to the masses and their well-being.

It also had the effect of limiting the size of the gulf between the élites and the masses. Thus. the concept had social utility just as the concept of family has social utility as a '*card-carrying member of the protest generation*'

Dr. Hamilton reflected when he observed:

> *When workers demanded a 'living wage' that could sustain a married man and his wife and children, the moral argument had wide appeal.*[100]

Partially, the answer to the question lies in Sig. Gramsci's conclusion: concentrate on the difficult and immensely complicated tasks that a 'war of position' within civil society entails.

Fighting a war requires bullets and, in a cultural war, those bullets are a set of coherent and consistent ideas. To generate and promote those ideas there needs to be created a vehicle which will develop and promote a coherent set of economic, social, cultural and moral ideas and policies based on a foundation which provides an alternative to both liberalism or individualism and to stakeholder capitalism. This would be a set of ideas and policies which reflects the values and lifestyles of the masses.

That requires a well-resourced centre of ideas or a think tank which is built on the foundations of Edmund Burke and Christopher Lasch and which develops and promotes a comprehensive and coherent set of principles and ideas addressing economic, social and cultural issues.

That leaves Sig. Gramsci and his focus on cultural hegemony. Along with the set of ideas, principles and policies, there needs be a strategy to promote them in academia, among teachers and bureaucracies and to

---

100 *Can Porn Set Us Free?*

advocate them in the media. The war also needs fewer would-be warriors haunting the corridors of accounting firms, barristers' chambers and the corridors of legal firms and more engagement on the less-salubrious but forefront battlegrounds of academia, bureaucracy and schools.

Removing the current incumbents from these citadels would be a battle akin to urban warfare rather than desert warfare. It would be a tortuous battle won step by step, street by street rather than by wholesale broadsides or a sudden one-off lightning strike.

While major political parties can be vehicles for the endorsement and imposition of ideas, neither politics nor major political parties are the primary tools to engage in a battle of ideas. The major parties respond to culture, they do not direct it. Political parties can provide useful platforms to promote ideas and are effective when they are part of a broader movement. That is a lesson to be learnt from the Greens who understand Sig. Gramsci's strategy very well, and are products of it.

A leader like former US president, Ronald Reagan, who understands culture wars and knows what role politicians can and cannot play and who has the will, courage, conviction and ability to champion a cause, is a luxury — albeit a very welcome one — but not a necessity. May be the Prime Minister of Italy, Giorgia Meloni, will emerge as such a person.

However, what would be more helpful in the war of

ideas is the thinkers to build on Mr Burke and Mr Lasch, and, of course, a conservative Antonio Gramsci.

The Voice

Beware the Shiny Bauble

Robert Katter

Introduction

The idea that there is a silver bullet to solving the deep-seated challenges and the lack of opportunities facing First Australian communities, especially in regional and rural Australia, while well-intentioned is naïve and ill-informed.

Having more people floating around Canberra purporting to represent the breadth of concerns, aspirations and challenges of all Aboriginal communities from Port Arthur to Cape York Peninsular would be just another silver bullet. Stripped to the essentials, that is what The Voice would offer if it were carried.

Like most silver bullets created by inner suburban élites in Sydney, Melbourne and Canberra the solutions it offers are vague and immeasurable. It could hardly be any other way since its designers, who live thousand of kilometres from the coal face, have little, if any, idea of or experience with the issues and challenges facing indigenous communities in rural Australia.

The proposal of the political and intellectual élites for The Voice is based more on appealing to feelings of guilt than concrete solutions to well-known and long-standing challenges. It is another example of the domination of policy and political debates by the beliefs of the inner metropolitan élites at the expense of people living in regional and rural areas, many of whom have a more realistic and informed appreciation of the challenges.

Presenting the Voice as the panacea to all problems relating to our First Australians is a cruel and misleading approach and avoids the great problems they confront. Not only would it reinforce a divided Australian culture, but it also would create an effective diversion from pursuing the true solutions to deep-seated and long-standing problems. In fact, well-intentioned people supporting The Voice often are the same people undermining or at least, holding back our Traditional Custodians from participating in the modern economy.

My experience of working with government in this space leads me to question what is the point of having even the greatest voice if there is no one willing to 'listen and act' at the other end.

A little personal background

My paternal ancestry follows four generations of Lebanese immigrants to Australia who immediately settled in North West Queensland around 1890 and have never left. I am proud to say that my family has remained egalitarian and therefore opposed to much of the accepted segregation which took place in our country's developing years – so much so that we still are described as being one of the first local family businesses in the small cattle and mining town of Cloncurry to employ Aboriginal staff in a store on the main street.

This was a very controversial and very deliberate move for my family at the time. My grandfather also proudly removed the segregation bar in the cinema promptly after taking ownership. I am deeply proud of these acts of equality and compassion on behalf of my forefathers.

My great grandfather served as a councillor in Cloncurry, my grandfather represented the Federal seat for this area from 1966 until cancer took his life in 1990 and my father served in State Parliament for the same area from 1974 to 1992 before being elected to the Federal Parliament where he remains today. I have served in the Queensland Parliament since 2012. The area has been continually represented by my family for 57 years.

A politician with these roots must gravitate towards the challenges in First Australian communities who arguably require more political assistance than any other group. I do not pretend to be someone trying to be Indigenous or act as their spokesperson, but simply a servant of them, heavily burdened by their issues.

Scarcely a day goes by when I am not in contact with someone from the First Australian communities or addressing an issue affecting them. I am proud to say much of this interaction is from people calling my mobile direct or calling into my office. I might add that most have little in common with the Indigenous advocates for the Voice to Parliament that I see on the TV.

From this vantage point, I confront the 'The Voice' with no artificial desire to satisfy any large guilt complex like some people living with the comforts of inner metropolitan city dwellers.

Coupled with this background, and perhaps more important, is my strong desire to live in the remote north west Queensland region with a very multicultural spine — a mining city attracting people from all over the world with a strong Indigenous population heavily influenced by its proximity to the Gulf Country and the Northern Territory.

The city of Mount Isa is a place where words are subordinate to actions – a perfect home for any politician wanting to curtail their own ego. I recall fondly a friend of mine who resides in a remote Indigenous community and who dedicates his life to advancing the people he lives with. He recently said at a public function that he would not do an acknowledgement to country because he lives by the mantra 'Deeds not Words' and if he has not done enough already to demonstrate his respect for the Aboriginal people then he should not be speaking at all.

In regional Queensland people do not talk multiculturalism or profess its virtues: they live it and get on with life. Consequently, I have a deep desire to improve the outlook for First Australians – not through words but via meaningful actions.

Genesis of problems - Stolen wages, economic rationalism

Before identifying the problems, it helps to understand their origins. I can only speak with some authority about North Queensland, but perhaps the principle in play here speaks for most other areas of Australia.

On reflection, the genesis of these problems originates back with the same cultural group that is now trying to rationalise and claim to repair the problems that they themselves created.

If you visited North Queensland, and particularly North West Queensland, in the 1960s and 70s you would have encountered Aboriginal workers and families on most large cattle stations. Over 50 per cent of the workforce in the railways identified as Indigenous and higher proportions in road crews.

Apart from mining, these were the majority of the major employers in the region.

If you visited now, you would scarcely find one First Australian family on the stations. The Queensland Government sacked approximately 800 rail workers from Townsville to Mount Isa and the Main Roads Department crews suffered a similar fate, all in the push towards privatisation.

The cattle stations were forced to lay off staff under Gough Whitlam who was attacking 'stolen wages'. While there was perhaps some good intention in this idea, the social and human benefits of taking in a population of 100 First Australians who were all schooled, fed and housed by cattle station owners to yield 10 or so workers were clearly not accounted for. When station owners were forced to pay full wages, the economics did not work, so everyone was laid off and they and their families displaced.

Those same people spent the rest of their lives pining to be back out on the stations, and my mother has personally recounted to me how devastating it was to see displaced families moving back into Cloncurry at the time.

This is not to say that there was not an issue to be addressed, or that historically exploitative practices should have continued unimpeded.

The railway workers and main roads workers fell victim to the economic rationalists from a government 2,000 kilometres away. They wanted to work towards privatisation of these utilities and services and replaced locally based regional workforce with fly-in-fly-out style private contractors that we have today.

These were decisions from disconnected government thousands of kilometres away that clearly had no idea and did not care about the social catastrophe they were creating for the future.

I could name families who were once led by very well-respected foreman, station ringers or railway workers who fell off the rails, so to speak. Their families have remained in unemployment and have been destabilised ever since. The human suffering that has resulted from these (governmentally-imposed) trends should be unimaginable in a First World country in the 21st century. Yet it is a reality for many of our First Australians, and one that I – as a long-term resident of outback North West Queensland and an elected State Member – regretfully have a front row seat to observe.

These decisions by both 'progressive' and 'conservative' governments are undeniable contributors to the high incidence of unemployment and subsequent chronic alcoholism and abuse that exists in Aboriginal communities all across Australia. They are also indicative of the preferred approach of out of touch metropolitan-centric political and bureaucratic decision makers who act based on how their decisions will be viewed by their equally ignorant and equally self-indulgent social circles rather than what is in the interests of those with the greatest needs.

Identifying the real issues

There are many basic initiatives representing the low hanging fruit for turning things around in Indigenous communities across Australia. Those that come to mind include addressing the effects of Blue Cards on unemployment and providing Title Deeds to enable home ownership on country. These are low-cost initiatives that could be pursued tomorrow, but seemingly would not generate the typical photo opportunities, warm inner-glows or Page 1 headlines that the élites, and many Voice advocates, so suspiciously seek.

It is not necessary to have a referendum and have a few more people swanning around Canberra to address these issues. The fact that, after all this time, these matters still remain unaddressed suggests that creating the Voice would not make the slightest difference on the ground.

The first initiative - Blue Cards

The first obvious governmental quandary impacting on First Australians in Queensland is the Blue Card system.

My recent experience in the Queensland Parliament with Blue Cards is as the strongest evidence we have that the current debate on the Voice is tokenistic, centred around virtue-signalling and is little concerned with action.

I would argue strongly that, for the large number of dispossessed First Australians, particularly in remote communities, their salvation lies in meaningful work – having a reason to get out of bed in the morning.

The most pervasive and prominent blockage to any First Australians accessing work in Queensland is the Blue Card – a card introduced primarily to ensure the safety of children from adult workers that may present a risk. Any offences committed by a person can be recorded, including offences unrelated to children, and remain perpetually embedded on their record. This may seem a fair proposition to most living in the city. However, an adult living in a remote Indigenous community, where social dysfunction, violence, poverty and criminality is omnipresent, is far more likely to have a criminal history or have come to the attention of police in some way

In a place like Mornington Island, for example, where, until recently alcohol was banned, the most common offence was homebrew production, which has little to do at all with the safety of kids, and this meant the offender would continue to struggle to get a Blue Card.

Without a Blue Card it is virtually impossible to get a government job. Almost every job in these communities is a government job with scarcely any private business or organic industry. Most jobs in these communities all involve some exposure to kids at some point. This means that gardeners, cleaners, builders and even sewerage workers have all reported that they have required Blue Cards.

The response of the bureaucracy is not to admit that the system is flawed and resulting in outcomes that were never intended, but to argue for more education and support for people applying for a Blue Card to help ensure they are successful in their application. Sadly, this attitude is a manifestation of the ignorance that created this problem in the first place. Simply put, despite governments best efforts they generally fall short of providing even the most basic services in these communities let alone providing additional support of this nature.

For ten years, I have sought to fix the consequences of the Blue Card system. That is to leave in place most of the regulatory framework for protecting children, including a complete ban for anyone guilty of sexually-based crimes, yet allows the local Community Justice Groups to make the decision in the interests of the community in some circumstances. To this end, I have tried to modify the rules around Blue Cards three times.

My proposal would allow an applicant from an Indigenous community who has been denied a Blue Card to have the final decision-making undertaken by a group of elders, local law enforcement and the local magistrate. This would mean that the local body that already actively works with the courts would make the judgment call on who works with the kids in their own community instead of someone unknown to them from Brisbane.

Given that no Indigenous community in Queensland

has a formal population over 3,000 people it is safe to say that the Local Justice Groups collectively know everyone in town. They know very well if a person represents a real risk to their kids working in a particular role in their community.

The existing Blue Card serves little purpose in Indigenous communities where everyone knows everyone and most, if not all, child-related offences are not occurring inside the schools or the hospitals where the card is required for work but instead at the homes or on the streets where they are not required.

The main consequence they have is to deny those people trying to turn their life around, an opportunity to engage in the modern economy. Idle minds and hands most often turn back to alcohol or drugs, creating a more volatile environment for the same child at home who is the intended beneficiary of the protection system.

This idea has grown in support amongst the Indigenous communities as awareness has grown on what the impact of the Blue Card has. Every mayor of every single Indigenous community in Queensland that I have engaged on this (which is most) have been nothing less than strongly supportive of this initiative. Most have now moved from a position of advocacy to one of demanding action.

So here were the combined voices from the mayors in the Indigenous communities in Queensland all presenting their voice to the Queensland Parliament.

Presumably, this is an example of what supporters of the Voice say it is setting out to achieve: to provide autonomy for and enable meaningful decision making by these communities.

Yet, the Queensland Parliament has voted twice on this proposal and twice Labor and the Liberal National Party have voted against making any changes to the current, flawed system.

Labor leads the cheer squad of the inner suburban élites demanding that that we have a referendum to appoint a few people, purporting to represent Indigenous people from Cape York to Port Arthur, to swan around Canberra doing who knows what, but never have they supported this proposal which would improve the lives and lifestyles of Indigenous people. Nor have they suggested an alternative.

One comment made by a Labor politician was "This was the right thing to do but you know how it is – we have to be tough on crime".

The most hypocritical and demoralising part of this exercise was Labor's argument that, if local indigenous leaders are allowed to make decisions, the safety of the children will be compromised and the safety of the child is paramount. This is coming from the party which berates anybody who opposes the Voice. Personally, I think that sort of thinking is racist, which is ironically an accusation made by many advocates of the Voice against those who oppose it.

The hypocrisy on other issues is not as acute but is

equally consequential. For example, the issue of Title Deeds remains another outstanding policy opportunity rejected by both Labor and the Liberal National Party.

Title Deeds

A cornerstone of capitalism is land tenure. Yet the opportunity for this in Queensland is exclusively denied to people in Indigenous communities. This must be one of the most reprehensible, prejudicial oversights in policies towards First Australians that remains deliberately unattended.

Proudly, the first ever Indigenous title deeds issued in Queensland were by my father as the Minister for Aboriginal Affairs in the Sir Joh Bjelke Peterson era. These were only available after his resignation letter was offered as an alternative to delivery of the legislation. These one hundred or so title deeds in the Torres Straits are to this day still referred to as the Katter Leases.

Picture First Australians in the remote community of Doomadgee in the Gulf Country of North West Queensland. They finally have defeated those demons of substance abuse and miraculously obtained a Blue Card. Once they have obtained a job, their natural ambition initially is to buy their own car. This may be followed by either purchasing a house or machinery equipment to start, say, contract work with the local council or perhaps cattle for their outstation lease. This person will approach the bank for a loan which will seek a mortgage security for the loan. Tragically at this rare juncture their ascendancy into the modern economy crashes terminally to the ground.

I know a fellow in Doomadgee by the name of Tony Chong who had an experience very similar to this. He owned his own machinery contracting business and had gone to the bank to borrow money to buy cattle but could not offer any adequate mortgage security. He was not aware of this barrier – only that he could not buy the cattle and progress himself. Here we lost a generational opportunity for his family and friends to see how there are legitimate pathways to prosperity in these remote areas.

Without land tenure there can never be any movement towards the modern economy. Rather cynically now the Queensland Government offers what they call Indigenous Freehold. Indigenous people clearly cannot be trusted with normal freehold, but rather an encumbered alternative that only permits them to use the land for a narrow range of activities.

Again, the subtext is that we will give you freehold but you are not responsible enough to be granted freehold that any white fella can get.

The 'why' behind the reluctance to providing title deeds to our First Australian Communities became apparent in a recent conversation with a Labor politician in a rare show of honesty and goodwill across the trenches.

I offered my view that it was important to try and provide opportunities to our First Australians to participate in the modern economy: wording I had in fact stolen from one of the mayors of a North Queensland Indigenous community. The response from this person had a profound effect on me that opened my eyes: "But do you think that we have to progress them? Shouldn't we just be trying to accommodate them in the ways that they are accustomed to like their traditional ways of hunting and living on the land."

I was confronted with the counter position to mine: that we should make racial divisions and leave one group behind to be treated differently by limiting their opportunities.

So far as I am concerned this view is racism. There are those that want to create or perhaps perpetuate a second class of people in this country and suppress them in terms of our modern economy. Maybe virtuous idealistically but sadly out of sync with a great many people in these communities.

I recall the words of an Indigenous friend of mine that served in the Queensland Parliament and who after leaving parliament said to me, "I now realise that I was always in the wrong faction of the Labor Party. I was in the Left and they are more racist than anyone. They still want black fellas to live under trees and chase goanna. They don't realise there is an emerging black middle class who want their own house and job in the mines".

We do not need the Voice to address these issues. In fact, passing the Voice could make situations for our

First Australians worse. It could provide an excuse for not accepting responsibility for addressing these issues by saying that it is now the job of a few people running around Canberra.

Culture

Invoking the word culture immediately provides a vague solution to a very complex problem that people can scarcely question, particularly non-indigenous people.

I was recently introduced to the concept of 'geographic narcissism' describing people, typically from larger metropolitan governing centres, imposing their values on others far away assuming they would adopt them.

An example of this seems to be the great divide between the contributions from First Australian Northern Territory Senator Jacinta Price and the typical ABC report from the Northern Territory. The sharp contrast in views was described to me recently by one Territorian who explained how the place is littered with well-meaning city dwellers from down south seeking to quench their thirst for social justice.

The cultural solution to fixing problems in our First Australian communities couples beautifully with the spirit of geographic narcissism. Many policy makers from our governing centres, be they politicians or modern academics, set policy to address these problems with culture as the centre piece.

This conflicts sharply with the words of one of our best Aboriginal leaders in the North West Queensland, Colin Saltmere, who said to me some years ago "you have to keep their hands busy Robbie". Colin, who is a traditional owner, developed and operates arguably the best training facility for Indigenous young adults entering construction or mining industries in Queensland, if not Australia.

Colin would make sure that all his trainees observe elements of their culture. However, this is quite different to making it the starting point in the pursuit of their work life.

Evidence of this bias towards culture as the panacea of rehabilitation was apparent in an exchange with one of the Queensland Government ministers over a new youth programme announcement in my region. In the briefing, the minister advised me that the youth can go 'on country' but they are not to participate in any rural activities like horse riding, motor bikes, cattle work or fencing. They can only participate in cultural activities for the days or weeks that they attend the programme.

These kids are intuitive. They know that if they are learning cattle work skills there is a strong chance that they can get work after the programme or as they get older. Giving them cultural activities is of some value but this simply has a full stop after it – what do they do with this cultural practice that will help them make a dollar?

This is not to say we should not observe the culture

of our First Australians. This is something to be greatly respected and admired. I grew up in a house with an entire room (the artifacts room) dedicated to Indigenous artifacts.

Proponents of the Voice assert that they are speaking for the entire Aboriginal population.

However, I listened with interest to a locally born and raised Indigenous Traditional Owner and a Gulf Aboriginal leader recently interviewed by the ABC. He said that no one in Doomadgee at all talks about the Voice. There are five priorities to turn things around in Doomdagee and they do not include this.

Culture remains the ultimate smoke screen for politicians and academics trying to solve these problems from thousands of kilometres away.

In conclusion

I speak only about the issues I know to demonstrate the hypocrisy and cynicism of political and intellectual élites who talk the talk and look through tinted glasses when it comes to representing the interests of First Australians. They do not walk the walk.

Passing the Voice might give Aboriginal people a sense that they have had a win, but regrettably this would be offset strongly by the opportunity it gives governments and the community generally to say that they have delivered while in fact delivering nothing material of any substance.

The value of the Voice has been profoundly tested by the vote on the Blue Card. It is a practical demonstration that the support of Labor and the élites for the Voice is tokenism at its worst.

I fear that, if the Voice did come to pass, it would darken any remaining hope of Indigenous people that anyone is willing to take on their problems.

One thing I know for sure is that, in five years' time, I will still be chasing the changes for title deeds and Blue Cards which are opposed by the same people advocating the Voice and Treaty.

About the Contributors

Rick Brown is a solicitor by training, having spent 2 years working in Papua New Guinea, 10 years as a union official and 10 years as the director of the Council for the National Interest and editor of *Australia and World Affairs*. He was Victorian director of the No Republic campaign, an adviser to an Independent Victorian MP and subsequently 2 federal Coalition ministers. He co-owns a government relations consultancy.

Robert Katter serves as the member of the Legislative Assembly of Queensland for Traeger, having previously represented Mount Isa from 2012 to 2017. He is the leader of Katter's Australian Party.

www.ingramcontent.com/pod-product-compliance
Ingram Content Group UK Ltd.
Pitfield, Milton Keynes, MK11 3LW, UK
UKHW020223250726
13967UKWH00001B/165

9 781922 815736